THOUGHTS AND PRAYERS
WEEK BY WEEK

THOUGHTS AND PRAYERS
WEEK BY WEEK

Lionel Fanthorpe

BISHOPSGATE PRESS

British Library Cataloguing in Publication Data
Fanthorpe, Lionel
Thoughts and prayers week by week.
1. Christian life. Prayers - Devotional works

All enquiries and requests relevant to this title should be sent to the publisher, Bishopsgate Press Ltd, Bartholomew House, 15 Tonbridge Road, Hilden- borough, Kent TN11 9BH

Printed in Great Britain by
Whitstable Litho Printers Ltd.,
Whitstable, Kent

Contents

Foreword

The life of a Parish Priest at its best has always been a very disciplined affair. Every day of his working life, he can be seen on his way to his Parish Church. Then the Office of Morning Prayer will be said, followed, more often than not, by a Celebration of the Holy Eucharist. In the evening he will be seen again back in his Church. Through the constant regular use of these Services, day by day, every day of the week, throughout the year, the Psalms of the Prayer Book will be said over and over again, and the Bible will be read almost from cover to cover. At each of these Services prayers will be offered for the troubled world in which we all have to live as best we can, for the sadness and difficulties of the people he is there to serve and has come to love, and for himself and for others, day by day, he dares to ask and expects to find forgiveness. He arranges his time early in the morning in the Parish Church in hope and expectation that some, at least, will be able to pray with him before they go off to work. So, thank God! they do. Occasionally, perhaps often, he will be there alone. And yet he is never alone and knows it. The Angels and Archangels and all the Host of Heaven surround him. He comes very close to the God who has called him into His service, a deeper relationship ever, day by day.

The author of this book, the Reverend Lionel Fanthorpe, will count himself among the most fortunate of men. In one sense he has succeeded to the best in two worlds. He is a Priest of the Church and it was my privilege to be one of his tutors towards his Ordination, but he has been Ordained to serve in what we now tend to call the non-stipendiary Ministry. He remains within the profession from which over the years he has made his living and brought up his family: in the main, that of schoolmaster and writer.

There lay his considerable gifts and he has used them well. In this calling he remains. Ordination to the Priesthood came late in life, but now colours and dominates all he does. He writes as a Priest; he teaches as a Priest; no doubt he sees everything in the world around him with the eyes of a priest. However, he remains, where he has always been, part of the world of commerce, industry and academia. The book he here offers is the product of his two worlds. He has learnt how to pray and he knows where he learnt it. He knows how hard others with their hectic, frustrating, demanding ways of life, continue to find it. If through this book he can help the "candle of prayer" to remain alight for more of us, he will be eternally grateful to the God he serves.

Canon Stanley Mogford,
Cardiff.

Introduction

This is a book for our *ordinary* days and the *ordinary* weeks of which those days are the building blocks. Between our feasts and festivals, dedications and anniversaries, birthdays and baptisms, triumphs and disasters, there are many *ordinary* weeks. The celebrations and the special days are the tasty fillings of life's sandwiches: the *ordinary* weeks provide us with plain — but essential — bread.

In a Ministry of only three years, Jesus did more for His Father's world, and for us, His Father's creation, than any prophet, priest or king who has ever lived — or is as yet unborn. That three years Ministry was packed with amazing events. Jesus healed the sick, restored hearing and sight, raised the dead, fed the multitude, stilled the storm, taught and preached, suffered and died, rose again in triumph and ascended to the eternal heaven from which He had come.

Yet Jesus experienced thirty quiet years of ordinary weeks as well. He must have been thoroughly familiar with the household routine of a first century village in occupied Palestine. What did He make and sell in the family carpenter's shop? How many times had He been with Peter and Andrew, James and John, on *ordinary* routine fishing trips, before He called them to be fishers of a different kind on a wilder and more dangerous ocean?

The Son of God, with a unique mission to fulfil, knew better than any of us how important the *ordinary* weeks were. If ordinary weeks are not filled properly, great events cannot take place.

If Jesus had not shown Himself to be a brave, loyal and reliable friend during their ordinary fishing trips might not Peter, James and John have made a different response to His invitation to discipleship?

If Jesus Himself had not invariably charged fair prices for quality goods in His village carpenter's shop, would He have had the moral authority to drive the money changers from the Temple?

If Jesus had not always told simple and straight forward everyday truth to His friends and neighbours in Nazareth, could He have delivered the sublime truth of the Sermon on the Mount?

So many of His great parables are based on everyday things. Where else would Jesus have seen those *ordinary* things except in His own *ordinary*, week by week experiences? How many farmers had He seen scattering their seed corn on good soil and bad before He told the Parable of the Sower?

How many flickering oil lamps had He seen go out for want of fuel before He told the Parable of the Wise and Foolish Bridesmaids? How many traders had He seen buying and selling industriously in the market place before He told the Parable of the Talents?

If our great occasions are the exquisite flowering plants in life's garden, then the ordinary weeks are the soil in which those flowering plants have their roots. The more carefully we tend that soil, the lovelier the blooms will be.

Ordinary Things

The church door sticks a little, and its key
Is stiff because I don't remember oil,
Until I'm there — and then it's much too late.
The hymn books, green and worn, wait like old dogs,
For owners who have promised them a walk
As soon as they have made a cup of tea
Or written one more letter for an Aunt,
Bedridden in a County Council Home.
Tyres on the gravel: that's our organist.
I hear him putting numbers on the board:
Two sets (one old, one new) which don't quite match.
Thank God for all these ordinary things:
The simple and familiar point the way
As surely as the altar and the cross.
I'll not get lost upon a road I know.
These old and trusted friends will see me home.
Our wise and loving Father put them here
For those of us who need their constant aid.

Lionel Fanthorpe,
Cardiff.
1992

New Year

We observe January 1st as the start of the year. We think of it as a time for new beginnings, for new year resolutions, for starting again with just a bit more strength and wisdom than we had in the year that's just ended. That's fine. Without a little mental stock-taking and a firm resolve to do better in future, we'd never make any progress at all.

The great thing is not to regard a new year as the *only* occasion on which we ought to make resolutions and try really hard to do better. Make the most of the calendar by all means. Start as you mean to go on —but remember that today and every day can be the first day of the rest of your life, if you want to make it so.

If things you'd planned to put right on January 1st are still dragging at your ankles like a ball and chain on January 2nd, take heart and make the most of January 3rd to start all over again. Those corrosively ugly old demons, Apathy and Despair, are two of Satan's most widely employed minions.

No matter what they whisper in our weary ears, this is our Father's world. He loves you with an infinite love: He possesses infinite power. There is nothing He cannot do for you. There is no problem He cannot solve.

Prayer

Almighty Father, Creator and Sustainer of all things, Inspirer of every new beginning. Help us to start again with You today. Forgive our many sins and failings. Strengthen us. Fill us with Your Holy Spirit. Help us to put Christ first, others second and ourselves last.

Give us new hope and courage with which to repel despair and apathy.

Give us the stamina and endurance we need to complete our present work, and the enthusiasm to look for more.

We ask it in the Name of Christ, Who brought His New Beginning to all the world at Bethlehem, and by His glorious Resurrection showed us the beginning of our own eternity. Amen.

Early in the Year

Outside my window it is January and it is very cold. Trees are leafless. Birds are struggling to survive. Skies are grey and heavy. Christmas is over. Spring is not yet on the horizon.

Sometimes my life feels like this, Lord. My spiritual sky is grey and leaden. My leaves have gone. No kindly neighbour has put out a few crumbs of comfort for me. Like Christmas, all my good things are in the past and I cannot retrieve them. I see nothing to which to look forward.

Lord of all hopefulness and all futurity, be with me on this bleak and ordinary January day, and teach me how to read it properly. Remind me that Your glorious and radiant sun is shining as brilliantly as ever on the other side of those dull grey clouds. Whether I can see it or not today makes no difference. The light is there. If I cannot see it today, I shall see it before this week ends. Teach me, Lord of Creation and Renewal, that there are buds on these leafless trees, and that when the times and seasons are right they will open into leaves and flowers.

These bedraggled and unhappy birds will sing joyfully again. They will fly. They will soar high into the sky. They will build new nests and raise their thriving young.

My spiritual greyness will pass. I will know joy, peace and victory: I know You love me, Lord. I know You care for me. I trust You to bring springtime and summer back into my life.

Prayer

Loving Heavenly Father, You are the God of the cold grey times which come in our Januarys as well as the God of our bright summer days. We praise and glorify You, Lord, for giving us that contrast which helps us to understand and appreciate every part of our lives. In summer and winter You are still our Loving Father. In spring and autumn, You are still our God. Help us to see beyond the greyness, Lord of Light. May Your light shine in us and through us, when the world is dark around us.

Remind us, Lord of all life, that greyness has its simple beauty too, and that the here and the now — the *ordinary* things of life — are just as much part of Your universe as the bright, exciting and spectacular things which attract our attention more easily.

We ask it in the name of Christ the Lord, who, for our sakes left the brightness of Heaven to be our Saviour amid the cold grey hills of earth. Amen.

Frost and Snow

There is frost in the air today, Lord, and snow on the ground. The trees shine like clusters of diamonds. The grass is crisp and white beneath my feet. The shallow puddles are frozen over. Their thin, cold, brittle coverings disintegrate as I tread on them. My breath, the breath of life that you have given me, Lord, forms miniature clouds as I walk.

How strange and wonderful is this world that is Your gift to us, Lord, where water turns to ice and every snowflake is a delicate gem — an emperor's ransom piles up in drifts against my garden fence. My dog is scraping at it playfully: happy and puzzled by its reaction to his paws. My cat leaves dainty shallow tracks, as she lifts her haughty, high-stepping feet and follows a line of arrows printed by a bold robin too wise for her to catch.

I learn from this frosty day, Lord. I learn that the most ordinary things — water and air — can be transformed in a moment. I see that one snowflake alone is insignificant but that ten million together can block a road or stop an express train.

When ordinary things do finally change, they change dramatically. When formerly isolated individual snowflakes land together they become formidable.

The cold weather this week has taught me more about myself, Lord, and more about those who share Your world with me.

Prayer

Heavenly Father, when the air is cold and earth is frozen, warm my heart. When the ground is like icy rock, warm my spirit and make me loving, tender and compassionate.

When I feel as helpless and insignificant as one isolated snowflake, help me to understand the formidable power of a vast avalanche.

Keep us ever mindful, Lord, of how fragile others are —like films of ice over shallow puddles — and help us never to tread carelessly on one another's dreams.

We ask it for the sake of Him who never broke a damaged reed nor quenched a dimly smouldering fire, Jesus Christ our Lord. Amen.

Home in Winter

Lord, I have locked and bolted my door, and drawn the curtains together. I have made a hot drink and settled down with my new book, my radio, or my favourite TV programme. My cat is purring on the rug. My dog sleeps under my chair twitching an ear occasionally as he chases imaginary rabbits in his happy, simple dreams. It is cosy here, Lord, and very comfortable. I am warm, tranquil and contented.

As I enjoy the cheerful security and serenity of my own home on this cold January day, help me to think of others: the homeless, the jobless, the sick, the poor and destitute, those far from home; those at sea; those working on oil rigs; in prisons; and the recently bereaved who are still weeping silently.

Show me how to help them, Lord. Teach me to pray for them meaningfully and often. Give me the grace to seek them out and share the precious gifts of human fellowship with them.

Help me to understand that You make us for fellowship, Lord, not loneliness; for sharing, not selfishness; for being together in love, not being alone in fear and sorrow.

I love the snugness and warmth, the peace and security of my home. May I always use it aright — as a place where I may re-charge my spiritual batteries and set forth again renewed, to do my best to serve you and my brothers and sisters.

Prayer

Lord, I praise and thank You for my home: for peace and security, comfort and warmth, and the loving fellowship of family and friends which means so much to me. Keep us happy, safe and well, most loving Lord, and keep us together. Save me from selfishness, and do not let me value ease and comfort so much that I forget those who have neither. Give me understanding, sympathy and true compassion, so that I may work and pray to help those who are less fortunate than I am. Help me to share happiness with those who have little or none of their own.

I ask it for the sake of Him who shared everything with us, Jesus Christ our Lord. Amen.

Winter Sports

Snowballs and sledges, Lord; I see them outside and on my TV screen. There are skis and skates, and exuberant children sliding on the frozen pond. There is intense activity everywhere: exhilarating movement and excitement all around. This fervent tide of movement is like a living prayer. Strong limbs and pounding hearts are praising their Maker by exulting in the strength and energy He has given them: *"All things come of Thee, and of Thine own do we give Thee."*

This is abounding *joy* in winter sports. We bring that joy to You, its Maker and Giver, as we remember the words of Christ: "I am come that they may have life, and have it *more abundantly."* These effervescent winter sports are tiny glimpses, minute foretastes of that *abundant life* which is our loving Father's will for us all. Show us how to take the exuberance and energy of our winter sports into the other areas of our life, Lord.

Teach us to throw away our groundless anxieties as easily as we throw away a handful of snow. Teach us to abandon our most cherished sins and vices as easily as we brush snow from our coats. Teach us to commit ourselves to You, most loving Father, as confident skaters and skiers commit themselves to the ice and snow-clad slopes.

Prayer

God of all power and might, movement and beauty, help us to seek and find You in our winter sports. Grant us abundant life in this world and the next. Give us the courage and faith to commit our lives to You, as a dedicated sportsman, or woman, commits himself, or herself, to snow and ice.

Help us to find our sure and certain goal in You, Lord, just as in winter sports we know our goal and strive to reach it.

We ask it for the sake of Him who made Calvary His destiny, so that Heaven could be ours, Jesus Christ our Lord. Amen.

Snowdrops and Crocuses

They are such delicate, fragile, courageous things: like John Bunyan's little blind daughter who brought him his food while he wrote "Pilgrim's Progress" in Bedford Jail. They push up blindly, but with unlimited faith and courage, through cold hard soil to the bleak white world above. And there they are: living proof of what indomitable faith and courage can accomplish. The effect they have on us is out of all proportion to their size. The human heart is greatly strengthened and encouraged by them. Snowdrops and crocuses are out. Winter's grip is weakening. Better times are coming.

The Princess Spring is on her way. Her surly old guardian, Archduke Winter, may delay her but he cannot stop her. He may hinder her but he cannot prevent her. The crocuses and snowdrops remind us yet again that light overcomes darkness, joy replaces sorrow and life is victorious over death. The gallant little heralds are abroad. "We are God's messengers," they declare with simple, humble, justifiable pride. "We bring you this news from Him. Courage and faith can accomplish anything. The frost and snow are passing away. Sunlight is returning. Life is re-awakening. We are here. We are the medium and the message. Here in this snowy garden, fragile as we are, we dare to proclaim the loving presence of God."

Prayer

Lord of all faith and courage, teach us the lesson of the fragile flowers that dare to bloom in winter. Help us to stand, with only our blind faith and courage to support us in this dark and sinful world of frost, and snow.

Help us to understand that any small act of faith and love which we perform will be conspicuous and as treasured as the first crocuses and snowdrops in a frozen garden.

We ask it in the Name of Him who came as Suffering Love to die and rise again that we might live, Jesus Christ our Lord. Amen.

Watching Television

The more closely we examine the components of everyday life, the more miracles we discover camouflaged by familiarity. The calendar showing the phases of the moon as well as the passing weeks is a masterpiece of mathematics; the clock on the shelf is a sample of precision engineering — even though it gains the odd minute here or there; the CD player reproduces music with an accuracy that makes earlier recordings sound like a conversation over a field telephone during World War Two. And then there's television. Through this small screen I can invite the world into my living room: and the world accepts my invitation. Gorillas beat their chests beside my china cabinet. Giraffes nibble succulent shoots under Uncle Kevin's wedding photograph. Kings and Presidents process between the bookcase and the coffee table. A battle rages near the flower vase. Pathetic refugees carry their pitiful bundles along a dusty road which runs between the calendar and the bureau top.

I can learn from it; laugh at it; be gripped by its drama, or intrigued by its mysteries. It brings me more vicarious life experience in an average week than my grandparents had in a lifetime.

Its potential for good or evil is vast; yet mine, as a living breathing, thinking human being is infinitely greater. Television can only *show* us things: I can *do* things.

Prayer

Lord of all wonders, maker and sustainer of everything our television screens can show, and infinitely more besides, help us to realise our own human potential to the full. Help us to enjoy our viewing, and to give thanks for all that is entertaining, wholesome, pure and good, informative, thought provoking and educational.

Grant us the gift of discernment, and the courage to oppose what is wrong and corrupting.

Help us to be men and women of action, not passive spectators in a world where there is so much to be done.

We ask it for the sake of Him Who did all things well, and Who did them for us, Jesus Christ our Lord. Amen.

Commuting

I catch this train five days out of seven. I use the same station and the same bookstall week in, week out. When nobody else has got there first, I sit in the same corner seat and look out over the same suburban landscape: rows of semis, neat little green-houses and washing flapping on lines.

We pass a postman or two, a milkman on his rounds, a police car on patrol, a cold queue at a bleak February bus stop. I read the headlines, chuckle at the cartoons and then settle down to the crossword.

Familiar stations pass between fourteen down and twelve across, and I discover with some mild self-congratulation that the answer to nine down (anagram) is that the clue "I'm a dot in place", (1,7,5,) means "a decimal point".

We arrive. I do my day's work and I'm back in the train. I'm going home, but I'm feeling rather tired now, and, if I'm lucky enough to get a seat, I doze off.

Commuting, like the crossword with its anagrams is part of life's pattern: loom and shuttle, warp and weft. There is a meaning to it — just as there's a meaning to that anagram. I smile to myself: I'm also a dot in place, but God knows that I'm here. I'm very small, but I'm part of His pattern: like the engine driver, the milkman, the postman and the people in the 'bus queue. He knows us all. He loves us. He made us, and he knows the true meaning of our lives. We are all infinitely important and meaningful to Him.

When the eternal solution of God's Great Crossword is finally published, we shall all know exactly where we fit into His infinite pattern of love and we shall be more than satisfied with His Ultimate Answer.

Prayer

Lord of all logic and all true meaning, help me to find Your Truth in the everyday patterns of my life. Show me how well spent hours grow into pleasant days, and satisfying weeks. Show me how well filled time is finally transformed into Your eternal bliss. I ask it for the sake of Christ, our Everlasting Priest and King, who gives infinite meaning to all that has been, all that is, and all that is to come. Amen.

Saint Valentine's Day

This is the season of St. Valentine, whose name is associated with love and romance. True lovers in each other's arms are undoubtedly sharing one of God's most wonderful mysteries. A man and woman gently touching hands and whispering "I love you" from their hearts are drawing closer to God as well as to each other.

Thank God for Valentine and all he stands for: unselfishness and purity, truth and gentleness; devotion and thoughtfulness. Surely our human Love is one of God's greatest gifts, and one for which we should never cease to praise and thank Him.

Prayer

Thank you for Love, Great Lord of Love. Thank You for those we love, and Thank You for those who love us. Keep us ever mindful, as we rejoice in our human love, that You, O Divine Love, are the Source of all abiding joys. Keep our earthly love pure, faithful and unselfish, that it may ever more truly reflect Your heavenly love. We ask it for the sake of Him Whose perfect love redeemed us all on Calvary, Jesus Christ our Lord. Amen.

February Rain

The old traditional country weather wisdom reminds us of "February fill dike" — and it usually does! It is pattering against the window pane and dripping from the sill. Rain is persistent: it probes every corner, every crevice; it gets blown under a loose slate. It finds its way down chimneys. It discovers a weak seam between the conservatory roof and the kitchen wall. It drips from the garage, where I should have had that old down-pipe replaced after I caught it accidentally with the bumper.

Sin is like rain. It struggles persistently until it finds our weakest point: alcohol, drugs, gambling, immorality, lying, boasting, greed, selfishness, pride, thoughtlessness ... Sin seeks out those weaknesses relentlessly.

But we are not defenceless: there is the umbrella of faith; the raincoat of prayer; and the tarpaulin of Scripture reading, to help us survive the dismal rain —until at last we reach that Eternal Kingdom of Peace and Light, which sin can never enter.

Prayer

Lord, help me to keep these very persistent raindrops of sin from exploiting my weaknesses.

Give me the powerful faith which wards them off; the courage and stamina to pray fervently and often; the grace to read and understand Your Holy Word.

I ask it for the sake of Christ my Lord, who was tempted in all things as we are, but Who never yielded to sin. Amen.

Shrove Tuesday

Pancakes: the feast before the Lenten Fast! There's something very warm, homely and domestic about the good old British pancake with its sugar and lemon garnishings. It takes me back a long time: clumsy, excited, happy, childish fingers (under a loving mother's guidance) trying to make a pancake leave its pan, rotate throught 180° and land safely in the pan again. (How *patient* Mother was, God bless her!) Partial success: about thirty percent of the orignal half-cooked batter made its way home — like the remnants of Napoleon's Grand Army retreating from Moscow.

Far too much of what we try to accomplish in adult life is very similar to our earliest efforts with pancakes. No matter how hard we try, and no matter how hard we work, things very rarely turn out in quite the way that we'd hoped and planned.

But God is there. Loving Hands (that still bear the scars of the nails) gently pick up the pieces of our broken dreams. The miracle of restoration is wrought once more by Patient Love, and we are free to try again.

Prayer

Lord of Patient Love, King of Restoration and Divine Forgiveness, please help us yet again.

We have failed You again; forgotten You again; denied You again; abandoned You again.

Forgive us, most merciful Lord, as You once forgave the dying thief.

Restore us.

Renew us.

Bless and comfort us.

We ask it for the sake of Christ our Lord. Amen.

Weekly News

Forty years ago, I was the journalist in charge of the Cromer office of "The Norfolk Chronicle". It was 1952 and I was seventeen. In a very good week we might just have circulated 12,000 copies, but I was inordinately proud of the job and of myself. In those days a young male journalist wore the mandatory trenchcoat and trilby — the latter perched at a rakish angle on the back of his head. It was also obligatory to carry a shorthand notebook and pencil, and to declaim excited variations of "Hold the front page!" or "Give me a scoop!" The only scoops I ever encountered in Cromer in the 'fifties were the ones that loaded chips into the newspapers I'd laboured so ardently to compile!

The reality was a million miles from the vision: catalogues of births, deaths and marriages, a local election or two, a comment from the clerk of works whose men were 'driving greenheart piles into a stubborn beach', a review of the local amateur dramatic society's production of "The Chiltern Hundreds", a few statistics from the National Savings organiser and a courtesy visit from the Captain and crew of HMS Cromer. As a perceptive poet once said: we were 'measuring out our lives with coffee spoons'.

The marriage of vision and reality is an explosive love affair between a vivacious Bohemian dancing girl and a phlegmatic, middle-aged archivist. Neither can ever be quite the same again, but neither can be happy without the other. The dynamic universe our omniscient Father God has given us is just such a marriage between mystical spirituality and romanticism on the one hand and solid pragmatism and logic on the other. I suspect that His Ultimate Truth is located somewhere equidistant between the two, and that each partner is essential to the other's very existence.

Prayer

Almighty God of Contrasts and Harmonies, Three in One and One in Three, Father, Son and Holy Spirit, help us day by day and week by week to understand more of the mysteries of Your Universe. Show us that what often seem to be paradoxes and contradictions in our eyes, are all safely integrated and harmonised in Your Great Plan — just as we are. When hopes, dreams and visions do not seem to match our everyday world, reconcile our thoughts to the reality that surrounds us. When reality seems drab, boring and lifeless, help us to energise and spiritualise it with our visions, dreams and hopes. Help us first to take Your world into our minds, and then to express our thoughts in Your external world. We ask it in the Name of Christ our Lord, in Whom True God and True Man became One Saviour. Amen.

Diets

Dieting, healthy eating, regular supplies of essential vitamins and minerals: they fill our consciousness this century as hunting filled the consciousness of the caveman. We are exhorted to eat more of this and less of that. Every week it seems that a new scientific report is published to arouse public suspicions that some hitherto innocuous ingredient (which most of us have eaten for years in blissful ignorance) is only slightly less toxic than strychnine, and we must eschew it at once or run the risk of arriving in Heaven several years early.

This is not to decry or belittle the latest scientific dietary findings: more fibre, less fat; more fresh fruit and vegetables, less sugar and salt; more exercise and no smoking at all. That's all eminently sensible, of course, and the loving Father God, who designed the human body and lent us one each for use while we're on earth, wants us all to be as fit, as strong and as healthy as possible. Diet affects the body profoundly.

But there are mental and spiritual diets to take into consideration as well which are even more important than our physical ones. There is nothing to be gained by having the body of an Olympic champion, if it houses the mind of a pig and the soul of a hypocrite.

Earthly dietitians may argue about the ideal balance of food, but there is no disputing what lies at the centre of the ideal mental and spiritual diet: it is Christ. We need faith in Him; we need frequent prayer, Bible reading and the loving fellowship of other Christians. We need to be aware of our own sins and genuinely to regret them. We need to be merciful and forgiving towards those who have sinned against us (in reality, or in our imaginations). We need the good, the pure and the beautiful in unlimited quantities. We need to cut out self-pity, pessimism and apathy entirely. We also need to take time out to aid our spiritual digestion, to saunter in the park and throw bread to the ducks, or corn to the pigeons, to watch butterflies on flowers, and squirrels in trees.

Prayer

Loving Heavenly Father, You know far more about our mental, physical and spiritual needs than we do. Teach us how to look after the souls, the minds and the bodies that You have given us. Help us to take care of others and to take care of ourselves. Show us what to seek out and what to avoid in every sphere of life. Help us to make the most of all that You have given us, that we may be whole, and that we may present that wholeness to You with love and gratitude. We ask it for the sake of Christ our Lord, in Whom was Absolute Perfection. Amen.

Lent

There are times when we have to do things off the cuff, to think on our feet, to make a swift, impromptu response. Sometimes those occasions are very successful — sometimes we think how much more could have been done if only we'd been properly prepared.

God knows when we're up against it, when the clock and the calendar are our worst enemies. He also knows when we do have time for proper preparation.

The unique events of The First Easter were of inestimably greater consequence than anything else that had happened in the entire history of the world. Only the Great Event at Bethlehem and the Second Coming can match the First Easter in terms of cosmic importance.

These weeks of Lent are our preparation time for Easter. Let's make the most of them in prayer, in Bible reading, in meditation and worship.

Prayer

Help us to get ready, Gracious Lord. Help us to think deeply about the meaning of Your suffering, Your cross and Your resurrection. Help us to turn meditation into active love, and so to keep a good Lent, for Your Name's sake. Amen.

Saint David's Day

Saint David of Dyfed (Pembrokeshire) flourished over 1400 years ago. The earliest written record of him (an Irish Catalogue of the Saints dating from about 730 AD) tells how he led worship with Saint Gildas and Saint Teilo. One of the most interesting things about David, Bishop and Monk, is his nickname of *"Aquaticus"* meaning "the water drinker". He was a great reformer, and, according to the early accounts, he would not permit his monks to drink either wine or beer.

He was a man of great goodness, kindness and mercy, who eventually became the Patron Saint of Wales. King William the First and King Henry the Second both made pilgrimages to his shrine. He is remembered on March 1st.

Prayer

Help us this week, Lord, to remember Your faithful servant of old, Saint David of Wales. Help us to remember him with gratitude as we recall the hardships that he and his monks endured for the sake of spreading the Gospel and helping the poor, the sick and the needy. Help us to be reformers as he was. Show us where improvements are needed in our own personal lives and in our world, then grant us the grace and the strength to carry them out. We ask it in the Name of Him Whom David served so faithfully, Jesus our Lord. Amen.

The Weekly Budget

In the days of the hippodromes and old time music halls, the stand-up comics used to make jokes about how hard it was to balance the budget, jokes which struck a sympathetic chord with most of their audiences. I can still recall the one about the lady who asked her butcher for a small sheep's head: "Please leave the eyes in — it's got to see us through the week!" Or the other cheerful but impoverished customer in the same butcher's shop who asked for oxtail and tongue in order to make both ends meet (meat)! The stout hearted survivors of that grim recession of the hungry 'thirties owed at least part of their victory over adversity to their cheerfulness and psychological resilience. For far too many people today, the weekly budget is an equally grim struggle. No matter how much care we take and how carefully we plan, there are always a few days left over at the end of the money. But God still provides as He did when Christ broke the loaves and fishes, or when Elijah was fed by the ravens. Our part of the job is to do the very best we can with whatever we've got: God will do the rest.

Prayer

Most bountiful and perfect Provider, help us to manage our resources well, whether they're great or small. When we have plenty, help us to give freely and share cheerfully. When we have nothing, provide for us from Your boundless store. We ask it in the Name of Christ. Amen.

Someone at the Door

Whimsical pseudo-scientific 'laws' such as the Peter Principle and Murphy's Law, embody the idea that if things can go wrong they will. One of my favourites is: "While carrying out an involved repair to a complicated piece of machinery, any nut, bolt, washer, screwdriver or spanner dropped will land (a) where it is least accessible or (b) where it will do maximum damage to the item under repair." Fanthorpe's Door Law is a humble addition to the advanced research already carried out by Peter and Murphy: " There is a positive correlation greater than 0.9 between a knock at the door and the following events:- (a) getting into the bath; (b) answering the telephone; (c) putting hot food on the table; (d) going to bed."

Our Lord's own human experiences of daily life gave us the parable of the Friend at Midnight (St. Luke 11 vv 5-10) who finally got the food he needed for an unexpected guest. Even a simple knock at the door has an honourable place in the Curriculum of Life — it teaches us persistence, patience and tolerance.

Prayer

Most loving and understanding Lord, help us to be patient and gentle, good natured and tolerant amid life's daily stresses and irritations. Give us a sense of humour and a sense of perspective, so that we may rise above the trivial and fix our eyes on the eternal, for the sake of Christ our Lord. Amen

Saint Patrick's Day

The Patron Saint of Ireland, remembered on March 17th, lived a very full and adventurous Christian life spanning the end of the fourth century and much of the fifth. Born at Bannavem Taburniae, somewhere between the Severn and the Clyde, young Patrick was captured by pirates and sold into slavery. After six years in captivity he regained his freedom, trained as a Priest, and returned to Ireland as a missionary.

Unafraid of hardship, imprisonment or the threat of death, he fought long and hard against paganism, idolatry and sun worship. Patrick combined saintly simplicity with true pastoral care, and never lost sight of his early years as a slave and fugitive — experiences which taught him to have absolute trust in his God.

Prayer

Most caring and ever provident Lord, help us to trust You day by day and week by week, as Patrick did. When drudgery makes slaves of us, and anxiety makes fugitives of us, give us the faith and hope he had, that we may share his Christian victories. We ask it for the sake of his Saviour and ours, Jesus Christ the Lord. Amen.

First Day of Spring

There is spring after winter; there is waking after sleep; there is healing after sickness and pain; there is joy after sorrow; there is eternal and abundant life after death. This is the message of spring.

"Behold," says God, "I make all things new." And He does: new leaves, new flowers, new life everywhere. The wonderful renewal process is ours to share. There is no admission fee. There are no boundaries or barriers of race, creed or colour. God's spring sunlight shines freely upon us all. God's gentle, refreshing showers fall everywhere alike.

The raucous and continual propaganda from Satan is darkness, doom and despair, death and decay. God's quiet truth unfolds with every leaf, and opens with each bud: "I am the Lord of love, of life and light. Spring is the letter Heaven sends each year to Sister Earth."

Prayer

Lord of the Springtime, renew us once again. Rebuild us, Great Master Craftsman. Open our eyes to see the colours of spring. Open our hearing to the music of birds and running streams. Open all our senses to the countless joys of mind and body which Your love has prepared for us. Open our hearts and spirits to a full appreciation of all You do for us. Fill us with praise and gratitude, for the sake of Him for Whom we give our greatest thanks, Jesus Christ our Lord. Amen.

Mothering Sunday

Of all the currencies and media of exchange which have existed since the world began, love is the greatest, the most valuable and ought to be the most sought after. Sincere, spontaneous gratitude is the only recognizable receipt.

It is not until we have grown up and become parents ourselves, that the full significance of parental love dawns upon us. There can be few greater joys, or blessings upon earth than the warmth, love and security of being brought up in a Christian home.

The love and protection provided by our earthly fathers and mothers is, even at its best, only a small scale model of the love and protection provided by our Heavenly Father.

Today we think especially of our mothers, all that they do for us, and all that their love means to us. The flowers, the box of chocolates, the Mothering Sunday card, the loving kiss and the warm embrace are only the stamp and envelope in which we send her the signed and endorsed receipt of our deepest and eternal gratitude. Thank you, dearest mother, for *everything*: may God richly bless and reward you for all you have done for me.

Prayer

Thank you, God of Love, for the gift of a mother's love. Help us to understand it, to appreciate it, and to return it. We ask this for the sake of Him whose loving mother once wrapped Him in swaddling bands and laid Him in a manger, Jesus Christ our Lord. Amen.

April Fools' Day

The best kind of humour (harmless, gentle, witty and free of all malice) is undoubtedly a gift of God. Cruel laughter and ruthless mockery are manufactured in hell and rank among the most vicious weapons in the demonic armoury. We are always permitted to laugh at ourselves: it is no part of the Christian life to laugh at others.

There are only two ways to try to improve our prestige and status levels relative to other people: the first is to do everything possible to be a better person, which is not only innocent and acceptable, but entirely praise-worthy.

The second is to criticize others adversely and seek to put them down — which is un-Christian, unaccept-able and often indicative of a small, damaged person-ality. The type of April Fool trick which sets out to embarrass someone, or to make him or her lose face, can never be part of the true Christian life. A harmless little joke or surprise which makes the 'victim' smile at himself is perfectly acceptable. The moral judgement depends upon the characters of the 'joker' and the 'victim', and upon the circumstances and intentions.

Prayer

Lord of all kindness, Who granted humanity the priceless gift of humour and the joy of innocent laughter, grant us also the gift of clear and honest judgement so that our laughter may never be cruel. We ask it in the precious Name of Him Who forgave those who mocked and crucified Him, Jesus Christ our Lord. Amen.

Palm Sunday

It was a big, public occasion. Garments and palm branches strewed the way.

"Hosanna!" they shouted. It was confusing, exciting, regal, epoch making: and very dangerous. The One who had organised it was the only One Who truly understood it. A few of those who were closest to Him had a rough idea of its meaning, but they were not clear about its full significance until years afterwards. It was an announcement and a challenge, a declaration, a demonstration, and much, much *more*: He Who had made the universe and exercised absolute and eternal power over it was here announcing His Divine Messianic Presence to the world of men.

There's one sense in which every day is Palm Sunday. God is here with us, right enough: beside us, above us, below us, around us and about us. He is closer than the air we breathe : and we are no more aware of Him today than that confused crowd was able to see Him for what He really was on the first Palm Sunday.

Prayer

Lord of all wonder, forgive our spiritual deafness and blindness in Your Presence. Help us to understand Your world and the important things in it, so that our comprehension of the meaning of events enables us to see You in the unfolding of history. We ask it for the sake of Him who rode into Jerusalem as Messiah, King and Saviour on the first Palm Sunday. Amen.

Easter

Life is cyclic. We climb its mountains with zest and then trudge wearily along its valley floors beside sluggish rivers that seem too old and tired to reach the sea. We abound with effervescent energy, or we drive leaden limbs with brains that beg to sleep. We have money to spare on Saturday night but we can't always find the price of a bread roll on the night before pay day.

When Christ was arrested in the garden of Gethsemane after the Last Supper, the terrified disciples forsook Him and fled. Peter, who was to become so firm a pillar of the Church, denied that he even knew Jesus. The wretched Judas lived only a few hours after the betrayal. From Good Friday evening until Easter morning were the saddest, darkest moments in the history of the world. *And then came the Resurrection*: the everlasting victory of Life over Death. The all powerful Christ, who loves each one of us with an infinite love, rose in triumph from the dead and is alive for evermore. *That* is the message of Easter.

Prayer

Lord of Good Friday and of Easter Day, be with us as life's cycle turns. Accept our praise and thanks when we rejoice and are victorious. Uplift and comfort us in our sorrows and defeats. We honour and glorify You for Your suffering and sacrifice on Calvary and Your eternal victory when the stone was rolled away. Amen.

Spring Cleaning

You wonder where all the dirt comes from. It lurks behind picture frames and on the top of rails. It creeps under carpets in spite of the latest technological advances in vacuum shampooing equipment. It lurks behind the cooker and gets under the fridge. It is not easy to deal with. It needs mental resolve, strong limbs and plenty of stamina. But once it's done, it's wonderful.

There are so many tasks in our daily lives that require the same sort of resolve, strength and stamina as spring cleaning does, and it's an all too human characteristic to try to avoid or postpone them. As with spring cleaning, however, the longer we delay our actions the worse things get. A firm decision and effective action will achieve the best results.

Prayer

Lord Jesus, You set Your face and went to Jerusalem, knowing that the agonies of crucifixion and the darkness of death waited for You there. Grant me a little of Your courage and resolve, my Hero Christ, to face my small problems as You faced Your gigantic ones. Help me to understand that the longer I delay, the harder my task will be when I do eventually tackle it. Give me the will and the strength to do it Lord, and to do it *now*. I ask it in Your Name. Amen.

Saint George's Day

England's Patron Saint was a Christian soldier who was martyred in Palestine, traditionally at Lydda which was then called Diospolis. He died at the start of the fourth century during the persecutions of Diocletian (284 - 305 AD). The historical George was a warrior saint, who gave his life for Christ — the most worthwhile cause of all.

The romantic legend of his rescuing a princess from a dragon teaches a different kind of truth. The real flesh and blood saint and the legendary dragon slayer were both heroes. The real man and the mythical man both embody great physical courage exercised on behalf of a worth-while ideal. George in fact as well as in fiction stands for the unswerving principle that some things are important enough to die for. Small wonder that he is the patron Saint of knights and soldiers, archers and armourers —and of England.

In an age of moral compromise, of weakness and retreat in the face of one social evil after another, Saint George is a vital reminder that God's people are sometimes called upon to fight for what is right.

Prayer

Heavenly Father, help us to remember that You are the God of Righteousness and Justice, as well as the God of Love and Mercy. Give us the courage to fight relentlessly against evil in all its forms, as well as the grace to work for peace. May we become as fearless as Saint George, who valued the service of Christ more highly than his own life. Amen.

Regular Worship

Our God, the Supreme Personality, understands our individuality infinitely better than we do. He Who revealed Himself of old by the Sacred Name meaning *"I am"* is a Personal God. The Maker and Sustainer of our universe is not an empty set of scientific laws, not a philosophical abstraction, not some sort of incomprehensible, mystical life force pervading everything else. He is God. He is Himself. He lives. He thinks. He feels. He loves. He knows. He acts. There is absolutely nothing which He cannot do.

Humanity does not stand in awe of science, philosophy or mysticism. It is a powerful *personality* that fills others with awe: we respect and admire the great scientist, the great philosopher or the great mystic. Even infinite power considered by itself is not overawing: He Who possesses and wields it is.

He Who is Ultimate Personality has given each one of us an individual character. A combination of genetic inheritance and upbringing, a mixture of what is inborn and what is instilled, makes each one of us a unique personality. Irrespective of how many billions of us share this planet — or, for that matter, how many billions of intelligent life forms may share the countless other worlds our God has made — *every one of us is different, and every one of us is of infinite value to our Heavenly Father.*

True worship is the sincere and earnest seeking of a right relationship with Him. True worship is an honest response to His creating and redeeming love. It may take as many forms as there are individual worshippers.

Individuality is not compatible with uniformity.

Two human beings who are deeply and sincerely in love with each other do not organise the expressions of their affection into repetitive ritualised patterns. They get on with the job of living their lives together, and doing everything possible to be with each other and to make each other happy. Forms, rules, regulations, patterns and restrictions are not the way of love for most of us; and yet there are those who find strength in regular orderly patterns and repetitions. God knows that that is the way they are made, and they are equally acceptable to Him.

If you feel God's presence in an ancient cathedral, go there and worship Him. If you find it easier to pray alone on a mountain top at sunrise, climb it. If you find prayer is more natural on your knees, kneel to Him. If you want to pray standing and facing Jerusalem and the East, do it. If you pray most naturally curled beneath your duvet at midnight, pray there in the warm darkness. If you want to pray for hours at a stretch, or at frequent regular intervals throughout the day, do it. If your style of prayer is a few snatched seconds during a desperately hectic life, make those seconds count. Worship is what we owe Him. Let us all pay our debts in the individual, personal way that comes most naturally, but let us never criticise our brothers and sisters because their ways differ from ours.

Prayer

Infinite Lord, You are Yourself, and You have made me what I am. Help me to find my true self, and then to use it to worship You in perfect sincerity. Amen.

Vets and Pets

Humanity's proper relationship to the animal kingdom as revealed in the Book of Genesis is a combination of overlordship, care and control. They are our responsibility. We are here to look after the planet on their behalf as well as ours. We are the stewards. They are a part of God's wealth with which we have been entrusted. They must be protected. They must not be allowed to suffer mentally or physically when it is within human power to prevent it. There is no Biblical foundation for vegetarianism, but there is a very strong Biblical foundation for kindness to animals. "Thou shalt not muzzle the ox when he treadth out the corn." (Deuteronomy 25 v 4.) The true meaning of the Sabbath and the real reason for the prohibition of work on that day, is to provide a well deserved rest for hardworking people and hard-working animals. It is not only the farmworker who is to be allowed to rest: the ox and the donkey are to rest as well. Those who legislate our Sunday Trading Laws would do well to bear that principle in mind. It was never any part of the divine intention to prevent a free man who truly enjoys his work from doing as much as he wants: work you really enjoy is indistinguishable from leisure.

For most of us today, the animals we know best are our pets: dogs, cats, canaries and budgerigars, even fish and frogs. Our world is unlike that of the Palestinian farmers and herdsmen of three millenia ago — but the basic principles remain constant: we are responsible to God for treating His animals well.

Our pets provide us with a great deal of love and companionship. In return they need affection, good and regular food and exercise, warmth and shelter, and visits to the vet from time to time for preventive medicines and treatment for accidents and illness when they need it.

Prayer

Most wonderful and creative God, You have given us so many things to love and admire in Your vast universe. We thank and praise You for all good things, especially the animals, birds, fish and amphibians which we know and care for.

Thank you, Lord of love, for giving us pets to love, and for the love which they show to us.

Help us always to show them kindness, gentleness and affection, and to care for them to the best of our ability.

Thank you, Lord, for the humour and fun which playful pets provide: for dogs who fetch sticks, for kittens who play with string, for lovable green frogs which hop into garden ponds and pools, and for the living lights of tropical fish in beautiful aquaria.

God of imagination and beauty, of love and humour, we thank and bless You for providing us with pets to love. Amen

May Day

Dr Brewer's famous old Dictionary of Phrase and Fable puts the origins of May Day celebrations back into the ancient past, with Roman youths dancing and singing in the fields. He also tells how early English celebrations of May Day associated it with Robin Hood and Maid Marian, and how archery contests in particular were held on May Day to honour Robin's memory. In Medieval and Tudor times, May Day was a great public holiday. People were up very early to "go a-Maying": flowers and tree branches were carried in procession, and maypoles were set up to be a centre for dancing.

What should May Day mean to the thinking Christian in the modern world? We of all people have something to celebrate. If we think of May Day primarily as a time of rejoicing, then we as Christian have more to rejoice about than any others. We rejoice in the love of God, the saving grace of Christ and the fellowship of the Holy Spirit. We rejoice in Christian fellowship here and now on earth, and we look forward to a joyful eternity of abundant life with Christ and with one another.

Prayer

Lord of the happy dance, Lord of all merry music and joyful singing, we thank You for times of laughter and celebration. We thank you for the gift of innocent pleasure. May we always praise and thank You for being the source of all that gives true delight. For the sake of Christ our Lord. Amen.

Ascension Day

Our Lord Jesus Christ came down to earth at Bethlehem as the Son of Mary. He undertook the most difficult and the most important task in history, completed it magnificently, and then went back to share the glories and joys of Heaven with His Father and the Holy Spirit. His love for us, and His interest in us is infinite, but it does not prevent Him from enjoying His rightful place at God's right hand surrounded by the priests, prophets, patriarchs, saints and angels who comprise the heavenly host. Jesus lived for us; toiled for us; preached to us; taught us His divine truth; died for us; rose again in triumph *and ascended into Heaven*. It is as simple and as magnificent as that. There are no ifs and buts; there is no room for trivial theological quibbles and prevarications; it is straightforward, Gospel truth — Jesus rose from the dead, spent some wonderful days reassuring his disciples that He was truly alive again forever, and then He went back to enjoy His Father's company as He had done since the beginning of all things.

Prayer

Lord of infinite power and infinite wonder, we praise You for Your Divine Majesty and Glory. Forgive our dullness, and our hesitant reluctance to believe. Open our spiritual eyes to the fullness of Your Resurrection and Ascension. Help us to understand that such is the Love between the Father and the Son in the unity of the Holy Spirit that it was only natural and right for God the Son to ascend to His Heavenly Home once more to be reunited with His Father, and to prepare a place for us. Amen.

Whitsun

How often have we prayed the simplest and most direct of prayers: "Please come and help me, Lord"? One person's phrasing of it may differ from another's; around the world and across the centuries, the language itself may change — but every heart that speaks directly to God with fervent sincerity and honest helplessness uses that same prayer. God's answer is the Holy Spirit.

Seek and ye shall find. Knock and it shall be opened to you. Ask and ye shall receive.

These are not blandly comforting aphorisms. They are not Christmas cracker mottos. They are not even the distilled wisdom of some great prophet or religious teacher. These are the words of Christ Himself. These are the veritable *promises of God.* He Who makes and sustains all things, He Whose love is so great that even death on the cross cannot block its path to us, has given these sacred and divine promises. The sun may never rise again. The moon may disintegrate and leave its ancient orbit. Mountains may crumble to dust and vast oceans may dry up — but the Word of God stands forever.

It is in the coming of the Holy Spirit, as He came to the first disciples on the first Whitsun Day, that the seeking, the knocking and the asking are answered and fulfilled.

Prayer

Come to us, O Holy Spirit of God, as You came at Pentecost, and bring Your almighty power to comfort and help us. We ask it in the Name of Him Who promised that You would come, Jesus Christ our Lord. Amen.

Bank Holiday

There's a wonderful atmosphere about a Bank Holiday. Some seek their pleasures in quietness and solitude, by lakes and hills, on lonely mountains and tranquil glens; others love to walk with crowds along garish, noisy sea-fronts, to eat ice-creams and candy-floss, to buy chips from a van, and hamburgers from a neon lit promenade cafe. Some would rather climb Blackpool Tower than Ben Nevis; some would rather ride a roller coaster at Southend than the Orient Express to Istanbul. Some are happier throwing darts on a funfair stall than watching Olympic champions throwing javelins.

We're all individuals. We're all different. We all like to spend Bank Holidays in our own special ways. God bless your quiet happiness tending your roses. God bless my day trip to Brighton. Jesus lived among crowds: He also went to quiet, lonely places — the hillside and the wilderness.

In the experience of the crowd, we emphasize our shared humanity. In the experience of solitude we emphasize our unique separateness. God has given us both. A Bank Holiday enables us to express whichever side our nature is calling to us most urgently at the time.

Prayer

Lord of crowds and solitude, Lord of the multitude and of each individual heart, be with us on this Bank Holiday, wherever we go and whatever we do. Bless us, protect us, and bring us Your eternal happiness. Amen.

Trinity Sunday

The idea of the Holy Trinity is not an easy one for a simple, human mind to grasp. We live our lives and experience our experiences in a three-dimensional world, where time is a one way process beyond our control.

If time appeared to us in different ways, if we had perfect and complete control of it — as God has — then it would be less difficult for us to comprehend the mystery of the Holy Trinity, of God the Three in One and One in Three.

Suppose that you are now thirty years old, the mother of two young children. The tiny girl you once were, sitting on your own mother's lap and gazing in wonder at your first Christmas tree is still alive in your memory and in hers, but she is separated from you by the passage of twenty nine years. Think ahead for another thirty years. You are sixty. Your grand-children come now to look at the Christmas tree. But you still remember your childhood and youth so vividly: the little girl of fifty-nine years ago and the young mother of thirty years ago are still alive in your memory, and the mother's love you gave your own children when they were young now lives in their memories too. They see beyond today's grey hairs to the fun-loving young mother who ran races with them beneath blue skies along a sunlit beach beside small sparkling waves. The Christmas child, the happy young mother at the seaside, and the sixty year old grandmother looking back *are all the same person*.

God the Father, God the Son and God the Holy Spirit are all the same Divine Person: absolutely distinct, yet totally united.

Prayer

Be with us, Lord of Time and Master of Eternity, Greatest and Most Holy Trinity, Mystery of Mysteries.

Reveal to us as much as our human minds can comprehend of Your Majestic Unity in the Fellowship of the Trinity.

Help us to take Your eternally loving Threefold Being as the perfect model for our human love and fellowship, that we may ever seek to blend our lives with the lives of those we love.

We ask it for the sake of Him Who said, "He who hath seen Me hath seen the Father," and Who sent His Holy Spirit to comfort and strengthen us, Jesus Christ our Lord. Amen.

Father's Day

C.S. Lewis, himself one of the greatest Christian thinkers of all time, once commented on the life and writings of the saintly George MacDonald. In Lewis's opinion, MacDonald's wonderful relationship with God was partly due to the mutual love and respect which he and his earthly father had for each other. MacDonald paid tribute to his human father by saying that he could never recall asking him for anything which he did not gladly give. Lewis commented that this also spoke volumes about the goodness of young George *who never asked his father for anything wrong or harmful.*

Our Lord Jesus Christ Himself revealed the true nature of God as the heart of a loving Father.

There can be no higher calling for a human father than to protect and provide for his wife and their children loyally and faithfully, to count his own life as nothing in their defence, and always to be there when they need him. In fulfilling such a vocation, a man comes closer to God than in any other walk of life.

Prayer

Loving Heavenly Father, we pray for all human fathers, that they may love their families as You love all the families on earth. We pray that their families may also love them and come to a knowledge of Your Divine Fatherhood through a proper experience of loving fatherhood on earth. We ask it in the Name of Him Who taught us to call You Father, Jesus Christ our Lord. Amen.

Midsummer's Day

There has always been a strange, magical quality to Midsummer's Day — even before Shakespeare gave us the mysteries of Oberon and Titania, and the fun of the clown with the donkey's head.

I have walked late on warm summer evenings looking at the stars in a June sky, wondering about Him who made them and placed them there; wondering, too, who might be looking down on distant Earth circling her tiny sun on the edge of an insignificant galaxy, and thinking about that One Same God of Everything, Who made his world and ours.

This is the day of longest light and greatest warmth; the day when our part of the world comes closest to paradise. Birds and animals flourish. Trees are green. Young fruit is growing towards the promise of autumn fulfilment. Midsummer looks back on the triumph of spring over winter, and looks forward to the harvest that is to come. Let us resolve to lead Midsummer lives today and every day: looking back at what is already accomplished, and forward with hope and confidence to the many great and good things that are yet to be fulfilled.

Prayer

Lord of all wonder and mystery, all profound thought and all true wisdom, help us to lead Midsummer lives so that we give thanks for all past success and offer humble prayers for Your help and guidance in the days to come. We ask it for the sake of Him Who shared all His thoughts with You, Jesus Christ our Lord. Amen.

Summer Holidays

While we're still here on earth the only way to get any realistic sort of idea of what Heaven is going to be like is to think of what we enjoy most here and multiply it by infinity: the smallest joy in Heaven will be better than that. To an unhappy schoolboy, Heaven is never-ending summer holiday. To the weary manual worker exhausted and bored by monotonous routine, Heaven is a free-forever deck chair and a really exciting book on the cleanest beach on the Mediterranean coast. Heaven to a red-blooded Viking warrior means fighting all day and feasting all night. To an Amerindian it's a Happy Hunting Ground. Behind each of these pictures, Christian or pagan, is the same basic idea: the infinite magnification of earthly joy.

The important fact at the back of all these pictures is that because God loves us so much He has two major plans for our destiny: He wants us with Him forever and He wants us to be blissfully, ecstatically happy together. True love has no other intentions towards the beloved.

The exact details of how our omniscient, omnipotent, omnipresent God will put His plans into effect are known to Him alone — but I know this as an absolute certainty: *He will succeed.*

Prayer

Lord of all true joy and of absolute goodness, may Your loving will be done for each one of us. Help us to fight against sin and temptation and to overcome evil by the strength of Christ and the Holy Spirit, so that we may come at last to Your eternal joy. We ask it for Jesus' sake. Amen.

Fairs, Fetes and Carnivals

All the fun of the fair: hoopla, archery, darts, rifle ranges, roll a penny, spin the wheel, knock down a coconut, swing boats, dodgems, roundabouts and try your strength machines — the patrons can buy things and try things to their hearts' content as long as their money lasts.

It's all very similar to the Parable of the Prodigal Son. Life was one big fun fair to him. Every day was a carnival — until his money ran out. Then all the stall holders who had previously been so keen to invite him over lost interest completely — apart from one kindly old pig farmer. (In today's rat-race, the Prodigal Son would have been very lucky to find one pig farmer with a vacancy!)

Bunyan gave us a vivid account of it in "Pilgrim's Progress" when he described Vanity Fair. Our word 'tawdry' is derived from St Audrey's Fair where they sold St Audrey's Lace — the quality and durability of which left much to be desired. Fairgrounds and carnivals provide us with a colourful microcosm of the commercial world itself: all its competition, pride and ambition in miniature. The wheel of fortune spins: nothing is safe; nothing is certain; nothing endures.

Prayer

God of the rock, our Eternal Certainty amid all that changes, give us discernment and sound judgment. Help us to distinguish between the vital and the trivial; help us to tell the priceless from the tawdry. We ask it in the Name of Him Who sees all things as they really are, Jesus Christ our Lord. Amen.

Saint Swithun's (Swithin's) Day

Saint Swithun was born in the ancient Kingdom of Wessex, and educated at the Old Minster in Winchester. He was Royal Chaplain to King Egbert, and responsible for the education of his son, Ethelwulf. When the latter acceded to the throne, he appointed Swithun as Bishop of Winchester (the capital of Wessex) in 852. Swithun was a good bishop, famous for his generous gifts to charity and for building many churches. Originally buried in the cemetery, Swithun's remains were taken to the cathedral on July 15th, 971. It was said that many sick people were healed on that day, and that it also rained prodigiously: this would seem to have been the start of the famous weather legend to the effect that if it rains on St Swithun's Day it will rain for the next forty days as well!

Most of us are familiar with the rain legend, but the details of Swithun's life, and the faithful and diligent way in which he carried out his duties are largely forgotten. Legends are sometimes like the cheap and garish covers of good and highly readable novels: we ought not to be put off by them, without enquiring further into what may well prove very interesting and rewarding.

Prayer

Lord of all Truth and Wisdom, help us to learn from Saint Swithun's legend that popular half memories may be clues to important facts about good lives well spent in Your service. We ask it in the Name of Him Who taught us not to judge others, lest we be judged, and to show mercy that we may ourselves obtain it at the last, Jesus Christ our Lord. Amen.

The Flowers of the Field

Patricia and I were in the Languedoc on one of our numerous research visits to Rennes-le-Chateau when we saw them: a field full of magnificent sunflowers. Every golden head was turned in the same direction to acknowledge the sun. They've been with us ever since, just as Wordsworth's daffodils found a permanent niche in his memory.

No matter how finely the professional botantist analyses and examines them for scientific purposes — and quite rightly, for Science is just as much God's child as Beauty is — flowers possess a sheer and exquisite loveliness which conveys a vital message. Can all this delicacy of form and colour, which is so breathtakingly beautiful, have appeared by itself as the mere consequence of a series of evolutionary 'accidents'?

Each sunflower soldier holds up the royal banner fearlessly and declares himself for God. Reinforcements of orchids and roses, cowslips and honeysuckle, bluebells and hyacinths turn their ranks into living rainbows. "Can you look at us, the King's Heralds," they ask, "and still doubt the existence of the God Who sent us?"

Prayer

Lord of all beauty, You taught us to consider the lilies of the field. Reveal yet more of Your truth to us each time we look at the flowers You have created. Show us Your power to save in the minute alpine flower sheltering safely between great rocks, for the sake of Christ our Lord. Amen.

Fruit Picking

It may be in your own garden, which somehow makes it nicest of all; it may be on your allotment just down the road; or you may have seen one of those familiar hand-painted plywood signs nailed to a gate, or tied to a tree, and reading "Pick Your Own".

You lift the leaves and search for the best fruit. If other pickers have been there before you, you study the rows like Napoleon surveying the battlefield at Austerlitz, before deciding where to begin. It's hard work, and the basket seems to take centuries to fill, even when families and friends are picking together. Then there's the constant temptation to pop the best specimens straight into the mouth instead of into the basket!

Gradually, however, the basket does fill. The first stage of the work is complete. Next comes all the careful preparation in the kitchen, and the freezing, the bottling or the jam making.

It is the taste of that fruit in the coming winter, when the picking fields are bare and empty, which makes all the summer effort worthwhile.

Prayer

Teach us, Good Lord, the value and the virtue of careful preparation. Help us to think and plan for the Eternal Tomorrow, even while we live for this day that You have given us. Grant us the Fruits of the Spirit — Love, Joy, Peace, Righteousness and Truth — here, now, today, in this world, and forever in the world to come. Amen.

Bible Reading and Prayer

On the famous BBC programme about the imaginary desert island the castaway is always allowed to take a Bible and the complete works of Shakespeare. If I was able to make an exchange on a three-for-the-price-of-one basis, I'd trade Shakespeare in for George Mac-Donald, C.S. Lewis and J.R.R. Tolkien. I would not exchange the Bible for every other book in the universe.

The Word of God has come to us through many inspired writers over many centuries. God speaks to us today through the strength of Old Testament Hebrew — a language described by one great scholar as so powerful that every word is like a coiled steel spring ready to strike — the beauty and expressiveness of New Testament Greek, and the crystal clarity and academic exactitude of Latin.

The Bible is not only to be revered — it is to be read, and it is to be read as often, as deeply and as prayerfully as possible. Bible reading and prayer are as vital to the healthy mind and spirit as food and drink are to the healthy body.

Prayer

Thank You, most provident Lord, for the wonderful truth the Bible contains. Thank You for the Gideons, whose work it is to spread Your Word so widely and so faithfully all around the world. Help us to nourish our minds and spirits every day with the sublime truth the Bible contains, and to pray for an ever deepening understanding of Your Word. We ask it for the sake of Him Who is Himself the Living Word, Jesus Christ our Lord. Amen.

Regular Sports and Fitness Training

A healthy spirit and a healthy mind deserve a healthy body. We should always bear in mind that the human body is also God's gift, and treat it accordingly. As St Paul tells us, it is the Temple of the Holy Spirit. It is in its own right a good and beautiful thing.

It is strange but true that many of us are more concerned about keeping a much loved car or bicycle in good repair, than we are about taking sensible care of our bodies.

We have already given a thought to the importance of a sensible, balanced diet, but what about regular exercise? As far as muscles are concerned, the old saying "use them or lose them" has a lot of truth in it. The more time we can find for sensible, regular exercise, the better equipped we shall be to live full and energetic Christian lives. We need strength and stamina if we are to work long hours in our Father's Vineyard.

Prayer

God of Power and Might, Giver of strength and stamina, keep us ever mindful of the virtues of training hard and keeping fit so that we can fight the good fight and strive without ceasing to make this world a better place. We ask it for the sake of Christ, Who worked so long and hard for us. Amen

Doctors, Dental Surgeons and Opticians

Just as a good diet, regular training routines and plenty of vigorous exercise are good for us, so it is equally important to have regular check-ups and preventive treatment from doctors, dental surgeons and opticians. If regular maintenance, valeting and MOT testing are good for a car, how much more important it is to provide the body with similar servicing.

Forty years ago, the great Methodist leader, Dr Sangster, wrote a sixpenny pamphlet entitled "A Spiritual Check Up" in which he advocated the practice of taking a little time out to examine our faith and our lives in much the same way that a good doctor, dental surgeon or optician checks our bodies for us.

Why not make a practice of asking ourselves whether all is well with our spiritual lives each time we visit a medical practitioner? Are my morals running at the right temperature? Is the pulse-rate of my giving strong and steady? Is my selfishness and greed as low as my cholesterol level? Does my spiritual blood sample show high enough levels of kindness, mercy, gentleness and patience?

Prayer

Jesus, my Lord, You are the Supreme and Perfect Physician and the Ultimate Healer. Take from my heart and soul the poisons of selfishness and greed, of cruelty and vindictiveness. Replace them with the fragrant tincture love and the world restoring ointment of a genuine concern for others. Amen.

Autumn

Crops are being gathered: pears and apples, corn and grapes. Leaves are falling and being swept into heaps, put into compost bins and returned to enrich the soil. The nights are getting longer. The dawn is late and the sunset early. The world dons a mellow mantle of red, brown and gold. It is autumn.

The year is well past its high summer, but there is still so much to be done.

The natural seasons are the mirrors of our human lives. When autumn comes to us there is still so much to do. There are the golden days of an Indian Summer still to enjoy — or St Luke's Little Summer as it is often called. Let us resolve with God's help to make the most of nature's autumn and our own.

Prayer

Thank You most loving, caring and protective Lord, for bringing us so far. Thank You for a life that has endured until its autumn. As we praise You for the colours and the russet beauty of the natural world at this season, so we praise You for long years of experience which have given colour to our autumn lives. Grant us the joy of Indian Summer, Lord, that we may still find much to do and much to enjoy in Your continued service. We ask it for the sake of Christ our Lord, Who calls both old and young, and uses the experience of autumn alongside the vigour of spring and summer. Amen.

Harvest of Land and Sea

This planet which God has given us provides an amazing variety of crops: corn and rice, potatoes and cabbages. Harvests come from land and sea, mountains and valleys, woodlands and open fields. Almost every corner of the earth has its own special contribution to make to the happiness and welfare of man. This plant provides essential vitamins and minerals; that one yields proteins and carbo-hydrates. Our Father is unstintingly generous, and the world He has given us is rich indeed.

There is far more than enough for everyone. If only we would learn to share properly with those in need no one would ever be in need. There is a mighty task here for the Christian as an individual and the Christian Church as a whole. Whether we perform the simple, personal act of buying our tea and coffee from an organisation such as Traidcraft which gives fair prices to Third World producers, or whether we enter Parliament as a crusading campaigner — as Wilberforce did long ago on behalf of the slaves — is a question of our personal gifts and our personal sense of vocation.

Prayer

God of the harvest and of justice and mercy, we thank You for all Your gifts, and we ask You to show us what we can do to see that they are distributed fairly to all those in need. Help us to take even more pleasure in the good things of life, which You provide so generously, by sharing them with others. We ask it for the sake of Christ, Lord of the Harvest of Souls, Who came to earth to share His Life with us. Amen.

All the Saints

Throughout the centuries, goodness and holiness have rightly been honoured, admired and held up to the rest of the Christian family as examples well worth the following. Some saints like Stephen, the first martyr; Alban, the brave and generous soldier; Francis, the loving and gentle friend of the poor, are very well known indeed.

Others, far less famous, are well worth remembering and copying: Adrian, Abbot of Canterbury, the greatest Christian educationalist of the seventh century; Donatus, the gallant and fearless bishop of Fiesole who founded a hospice for pilgrims; Ephrem, head of the Cathedral School at Nisibis in Mesopotamia, who organised help for famine victims; Fidelis of Sigmaringen, the great Capuchin preacher who worked tirelessly among the sick and suffering; Wulfram, the courageous missionary; and Zita of Monsagrati, who expressed her faith by a lifetime of patient, loving and dedicated service to the family for whom she worked. And then there are the secret saints: known only to God and those to whom they give their help: those who go without in order to give to others; those who spend their time visiting the sick and lonely; dedicated doctors; caring nurses and auxiliary helpers.

Prayer

God of holiness and love, help us to follow the example of all good men and women throughout the ages, and to worship You most truly by continual acts of kindness to our neighbours. We ask it for the sake of Christ our Lord, whom all the saints adore. Amen.

Guy Fawkes' Day

Many of our happiest childhood memories are associated with firework displays, hot sausages between slices of bread, and a large bonfire. Quite who Guy Fawkes actually was, what he had attempted to do, when and why, had little or no part in our childhood celebrations.

Born to Protestant parents in 1570, Guy Fawkes was educated at York Free School. After his father, Edward, died, his mother married again, and Guy's new step-father was a Roman Catholic. The lad soon became a devout and enthusiastic adherent as well, and served in the Spanish army when they captured Calais in 1596. His military experience, confidence, ability and enthusiasm led to his selection for the key role in the Gunpowder Plot. The rest is history. The atrocity that so nearly happened; the courage of Guy Fawkes while being interrogated under severe torture; the fanaticism and ruthlessness of the plotters and their opponents — all these things are a million light years away from boys and girls innocently enjoying a firework display.

Let us resolve to keep all that contributes to our happy, harmless, bonfire night fun, and to reject all that is fanatical, vicious and cruel — from whichever side of any religious controversy it may originate.

Prayer

Lord of justice and mercy, preserve us always from the deadly and fanatical delusion that we can achieve good by doing evil. We ask it in the Name of Christ our Lord, Who won the greatest victory in history with purity, truth and courage. Amen.

Remembrance Day

We need not confine our acts of prayerful remembrance to the gallant heroes and heroines who gave their lives in two world wars, and in the equally fierce, if more localised, conflicts that have arisen since. All who have given their lives for a worthwhile cause, for Christ, for the Church, or for other people are more than worthy of our prayers and our solemn remembrance: the fireman trying to save someone from a blazing building; the winchman from the helicopter; the lifeboatman; the police officer who dies on patrol, making the streets safer for all of us. War is savage and brutal. It brings out the worst in some — and the best in others, but it is not quite the worst thing in the world. Standing by and doing nothing while the innocent suffer is worse than war. Taking up arms is the last resort: but it is still a valid resort.

Violence by the criminal individual — or criminal nation — is qualitatively different from the fully justifiable force which has to be used by those controlling criminal individuals and criminal nations. The framework of society itself is threatened when that issue is clouded.

Prayer

God of justice, clear our minds about the issues of peace and war, violence and crime, and the work of those who protect us from evil. Help us to understand that although peace should always be our aim and our ideal, it may sometimes be necessary to fight and die for what is right. We ask it in the Name of Christ Who gave His life for us all. Amen.

Advent

There was once a tradition that the four Sundays of Advent should be used to preach on the themes of Death, Judgment, Heaven and Hell. Times change. The needs of congregations change. But there is still a lot of mileage left in that sound traditional idea. Unless medical science and technology move exponentially and at a speed which they have never achieved before, death will be the fate of our generation as inexorably as it visited Chaldean Kings and Egyptian Pharaohs.

The First Easter Morning destroyed the power of death: Christ arose victorious and lives forever. Death is now only the mysterious, dark doorway beyond which Christ is waiting to welcome us bearing the gift of abundant and eternal life.

But what of Judgment? God's absolute goodness, purity and perfection are inseparable from His fairness and justice. Christ Himself has told us that He did not come to destroy the Law, but to fulfil it. How can divine law be fulfilled by the exercise of love, mercy and forgiveness? Is a sadistic and unrepentant mass murderer to stroll into Heaven alongside Saint John, Saint Francis, Doctor Livingstone, Hudson Taylor and Mother Teresa? A gulf as wide as that is beyond the bridging power of any human intellect: but it is not beyond the infinite power of God. I cannot adequately explain the origin and nature of evil, its fatal grip on humanity, and its repercussive tragedies: but my God and Father can, and I am utterly content to trust Him not only to explain it but to sweep it away forever. Christ's suffering and death, His resurrection and ascension, and His eternal role as our Great High Priest (Supreme Leader of the Order of Melchisedek): all these are vital clues to the mystery of God's perfect reconciliation of love and mercy with justice and judgment.

Heaven is brighter and more beautiful than human eyes can bear to see. Its joys are greater than mortal hearts can contain. We shall share it forever with God and with one another. I know nothing of its details. I know only that it will be an infinitely prolonged experience of happiness and excitement far greater than anything that we have ever experienced on earth.

Hell is Heaven's foully blighted opposite. It is bleak, negative and nihilistic. The pits and caverns of misery and suffering it contains are unfathomable. It is the absence of joy just as cold is the absence of heat, or darkness is the absence of light. Our Lord Himself warned us very solemnly of its existence: and anything He says is good enough for me. If Christ saw fit to describe the horrors of Hell and warn us of them — then Hell is both real and infinitely terrible.

Prayer

Lord, at this Advent season, help us to think very seriously about Your coming to earth — first as our Redeemer at Bethlehem and Calvary, and secondly as our all-knowing Judge at the end of the world.

Help us to face death without fear in the knowledge of Your resurrection. Help us to face judgment without fear in the knowledge of Your love and mercy. Help us to find Heaven by Your grace and forgiveness, and to avoid Hell by Your constant inspiration and guidance.

We ask it in the Name of Him Who suffered death, gives perfect judgement, opens the doors of Heaven, and delivers us from Hell, Jesus Christ our Lord. Amen.

The Letter to Santa Claus

There is a story told of a very poor boy who wrote a letter to Santa Claus. In it, the lad asked for £5 to buy food and warm clothes for his parents and younger brothers and sisters. The letter was opened by the member of Post Office staff who happened to be dealing with the pile of Santa Claus mail on that early December day. He was touched by the boy's hardships and by his concern for his family. Several Post Office staff contributed to a collection to make the lad's dream of a £5 note come true. They raised £4.50 and complete with a short 'reply from Santa' wishing the family well, it was duly dropped through the boy's letter box. Next day another letter arrived for Santa Claus: "Thank you so much for the £5, but you'll be sorry to hear that some thief in the Post Office stole 50p before it got here."

When our Lord taught us not to judge others, He had that kind of mistake in mind. We know so little even about ourselves that we are in no position to condemn anyone else. God alone has that knowledge, and He much prefers to exercise His infinite mercy.

Prayer

Lord of all goodness and generosity, inspire us to be mindful of the needs of others not only as Christmas, the season of goodwill, approaches, but throughout the whole year. Remind us constantly that our task is not to judge others, but to help them in every way we can. Teach us to be grateful for what we have received, and not to complain because we had hoped for more. We ask it in the Name of Christ our Lord. Amen.

The Shortest Day

This week contains the shortest day, the start of winter. If I knew that this shortest day was to be my last day on earth, how would I choose to spend it? I should want to make my final peace with God, and to spend every last remaining minute in the company of those I love most, cramming in as many as we could of the things we have always enjoyed doing together: I would stand for the last time in the pulpit of my Church, and preach my farewell sermon; write my last short story (one with a moral) — followed by my last poem (one with a message). I would swim one more length of the Cardiff Empire Pool; get my weights out and try once more for the highest poundage I have ever lifted; play a final game of chess; put my judo suit on and fight one last fight. After that I would eat the biggest T-bone steak I could buy (dripping with butter and buried under garlic). I would play a final tune on my keyboard, and drink coffee loaded with cream and sugar. At five minutes to midnight I would thank God for all His gifts, and for the life that I had enjoyed so much. I would thank my beloved wife and my daughters for all that they had done for me, tell them once more how much I loved them, and how, trusting in God's mercy and Christ's Atonement on the Cross, I should see them again on the Great Day — and then I should be ready for the Eternal Adventure to begin.

Prayer

Teach us, Lord of Abundant Life, to live each day to the full, as though it were our last. Help us to make even the shortest day into a glorious adventure, with Christ at the centre and those we love around us. We ask it for Jesus' sake. Amen.

Christmas

If we needed any further evidence about the importance of Christmas, what about this? *"One way to assess the significance of an event is to count the number of worthwhile ideas and consequences which that event is able to generate."*

The Incarnation, the coming to earth of God Himself in human form on the first Christmas Day, has generated more worthwhile consequences and inspired more significant ideas than any other event before or since. God has broken into history to put things right for us. That is the true and eternal meaning of Christmas. There is infinite power to heal and save in the Babe in the manger. Sin is conquered. Death is conquered. Satan is conquered. And the Conqueror lies asleep in Mary's loving arms.

Prayer

God our Father, we thank You for the gift of Your only begotten Son, Jesus Christ, to be our Elder Brother, Friend and Saviour. May we go to the manger too and kneel there to welcome Him with the Magi and the Shepherds.

May we learn there to love Him as He deserves, and to serve Him faithfully in this world and the next.

We ask it for the sake of Heaven's Glorious King, who once shared a stable with oxen and donkeys, in order to come to earth to be with us on that First Christmas Day, Jesus Christ our Lord. Amen.

A Visit to the Pantomime

Whether it's Aladdin or Cinderella, Puss in Boots or Jack and the Beanstalk, the Christmas and New Year holidays aren't really complete without that annual visit to the pantomime. I think I saw my first pantomime in 1936, but I don't remember many of the details of that one!

Why is a pantomime so entertaining? What is the serious point that comes out through all the fun and laughter? It is the eternal triumph of good over evil: the wicked stepmother, the cruel witch, the ogre, the demon, or king rat —whoever the personification of evil is in that particular story — it is always defeated by good. Truth overcomes lies. Honesty conquers deceitfulness. Light beats darkness. Order subdues chaos and anarchy. All ends well, and the heroes and heroines live happily every after. Through the colour, the music, the clowning and the slapstick nonsense with paint, pastry and buckets of water, the real message of life comes through loud and clear. No matter what happens on the way — Good will win in the end.

Prayer

God of joy and laughter, come with us to the pantomime again this year. Share our pleasures, just as fully as You support and comfort us through our sorrows. Be with us when life is happy and bright, just as You are our unfailing support through dull days, failures and disappointments. Remind us that beneath the comedy there is eternal truth: the everlasting triumph of Good over evil. We ask it in the Name of Christ, our Conquering Saviour King. Amen.